Let's Remember....

INDIANS OF TEXAS

Written and illustrated by Betsy Warren

1981 • HENDRICK-LONG PUBLISHING COMPANY • DALLAS

CONTENTS

The FIRST PEOPLE

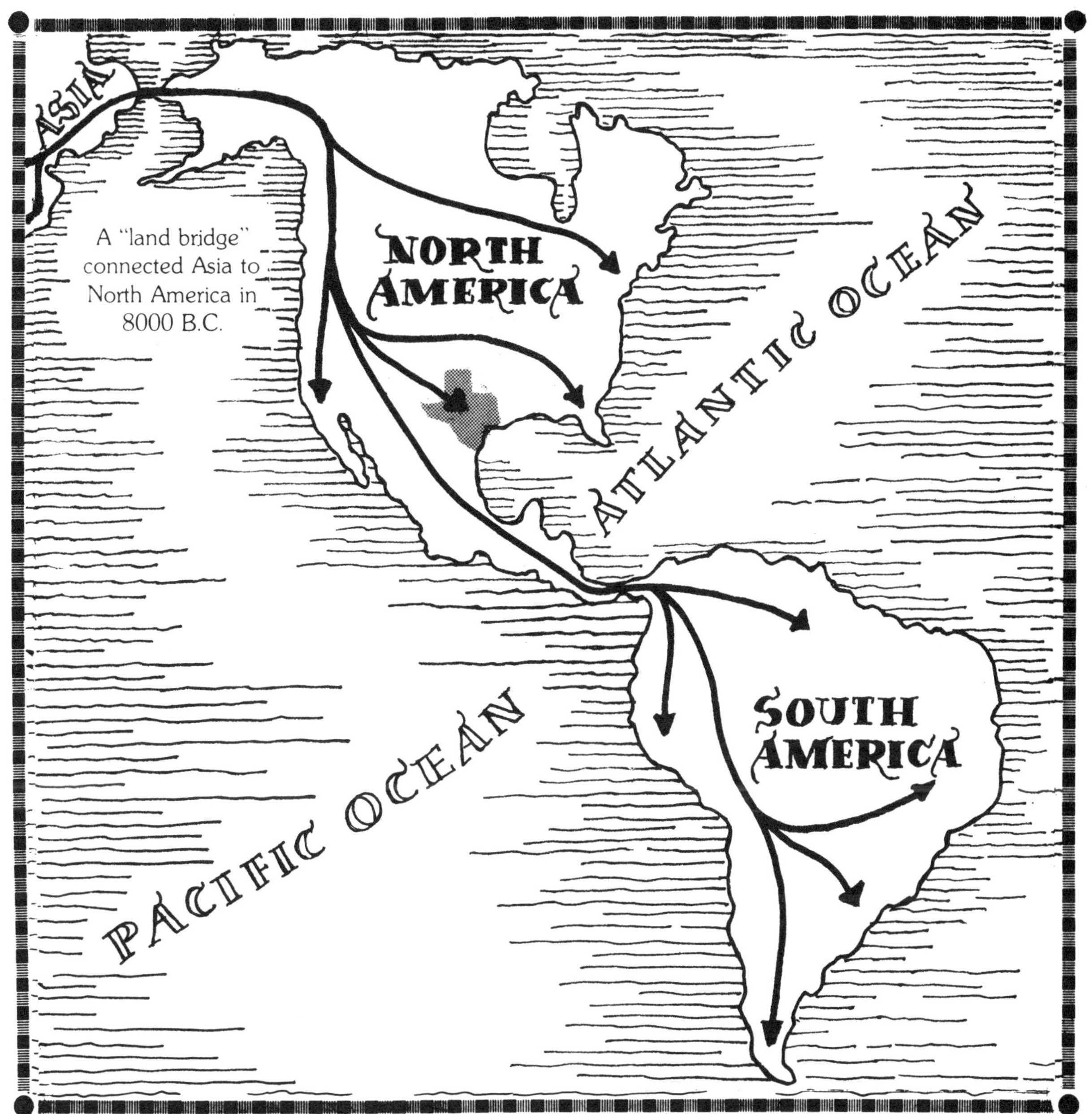

INDIANS were the first people who lived in Texas. We think they came from Asia about 38,000 years ago.

The WANDERERS

Small groups of Indians wandered over the land hunting animals and plants for food. For their weapons they used heavy stones or long spears. They wore animal skins for warmth and found shelter in caves near rivers and creeks.

After many years, the Indians learned to make bows and arrows. They cut the bows from tree branches and chipped sharp points on small flint rocks to make arrow heads.

With bows and arrows, Indians became more successful hunters.

The early Indians in Texas had never seen cows or horses. They did not know about wheels either. So they had to walk everywhere they went.

They used dogs, the first tame animals, to carry baggage on hunting trips.

The FARMERS

About 2000 years ago, some groups of Indians learned how to plant seeds to grow crops. They settled in villages near their fields and became the first farmers in Texas. Corn, pumpkins, beans, and squash were their best crops.

Berries, nuts, and peaches grew wild in Texas. The farming Indians enjoyed all of these foods as well as the honey they found in hollow trees.

Tribes of Caddo (CAH-doh) and Wichita (WEE-chee-tah) Indians lived as farmers in East Texas. Since there was usually enough rain for their crops, these Indians had plenty to eat. Corn was the most important crop. It was ground into flour to make bread.

Farming Indians of East Texas lived in huts which looked like tall beehives. They tied bundles of dried grass to a circle of tall cedar poles which were tied together at the top.

Each family had one large hut for its home and two smaller ones for places to work and store food.

In West Texas, Jumano (hoo-MAH-no) Indians were farmers along the Rio Grande. Like the Indians in East Texas, they grew corn and other vegetables. When food was scarce, the men walked north through the Davis mountains to hunt for deer, bear, and buffalo.

Jumanos built houses of stones or of adobe. Some of the adobe houses had two stories.

Adobe is a mixture of grass, ashes, dirt, and water which hardens in the sun.

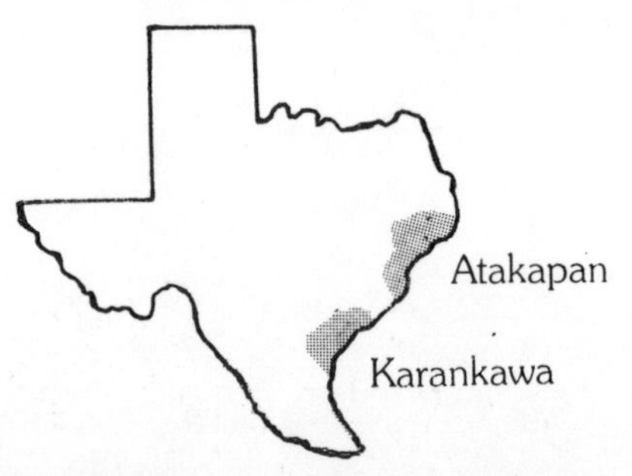

The FISHERMEN

Small groups of Karankawa (kah-RHAN-kah-wuh) Indians lived along the Gulf coast. The Atakapans (ah-TACK-ah-pahns) lived north of them. They all hunted for fish, oysters, turtles, and roots along the shore. Their canoes, called "dug-outs," were tree trunks which the Indians hollowed out by scraping or burning the insides.

Fishing tribes camped in shelters that could be quickly built of branches with animal hides thrown over the top.

Karankawas were tall, well-built people. It was the custom for Karankawa men to wear a piece of cane pushed through holes made in their lower lips and on each side of their chests.

The fishing Indians smeared themselves with alligator grease as protection against hordes of mosquitoes and other insects which swarmed near the ocean bays and inlets.

Atakapans were short and stout with bushy hair. They wore clothes made of animal skins and furs. The women wore skirts of deer skin and shawls of Spanish moss.

The PLANT GATHERERS

Along the creeks and rivers of Central and South Texas there lived tribes of Tonkawa (TOHNK-ah-wuh) and Coahuiltecan (co-ah-weel-TEK-ahn) Indians. They walked constantly over the land hunting plants and small animals for food. They built temporary camps of brush and moss.

Prickly pear cactus was the favorite food of plant-gathering Indians. The ripe, red fruit and also the green pads were eaten after the prickly spines were cut or burned off.

The BUFFALO HUNTERS

Kiowa (KEE-o-wuh), Apache (ah-PAH-chee) and Comanche (coe-MAHN-chee) Indians roamed over the plains of West and North Texas. They were hunting the great herds of buffalo which pastured on the plains. Indians killed buffalo for food and used the hides to make clothes and tepees.

To make tepees, the women sewed buffalo hides together. They threw the hides over tall poles which had been tied together at the top to form a cone shape. When the tribes moved to a new camp site, they rolled the hides on the poles and carried them along to be used in the new camp.

The Plains Indians seldom ate vegetables or fish. They did not eat bear meat but used the bear fat for grease and seasoning in their cooking. A kind of sausage, called pemmican, was made of dried buffalo meat mixed with berries, nuts, and fat. Pemmican was carried to be eaten on long trips because it did not spoil easily.

INDIAN CUSTOMS

In some ways, Texas Indian tribes were different from each other. They built different kinds of homes. They spoke different languages. Each tribe had its own laws, its own songs, stories, and dances. Each tribe also had its own way of worshipping the gods it believed in.

But in many ways, Texas Indians were alike. Even though their languages were different, they could understand each other by means of a sign language—making signs for words with their fingers and arms.

All of the Texas Indians were good hunters with bows, arrows, and spears. They knew how to make fire and how to cut down trees with sharp stones. They made baskets and other utensils from trees, plants, and clay.

All Texas Indians painted and tattooed their skins with designs. Shells, bones, animal teeth, seeds, and feathers were used as decoration. Texas Indians also liked to paint designs on cave walls and small rocks.

Texas Indians had no alphabet and no books. Older men in the tribes taught history, customs, and folk tales to the children.

All tribes held dances and festivals and made music. Drums of animal skins stretched over wooden frames, flutes of eagle bones, and rattles of gourds or turtle shells filled with seeds were their musical instruments.

The COMING *of the* WHITE MAN

White men from Europe came to Texas more than 450 years ago. They brought horses, cows, and wheels. This caused the life of Indian people to change. The Indians learned to ride horses and became fine horsemen.

Since Indians could not accept the ways of the white men, they fought with the Europeans and tried to keep them out of Texas. But they caught the diseases of the white settlers and thousands of them died. By the 1900s, disease and wars had wiped out almost all of the Indians who had lived in Texas. The few who were left drifted into Mexico or went to live on reservations in the United States.

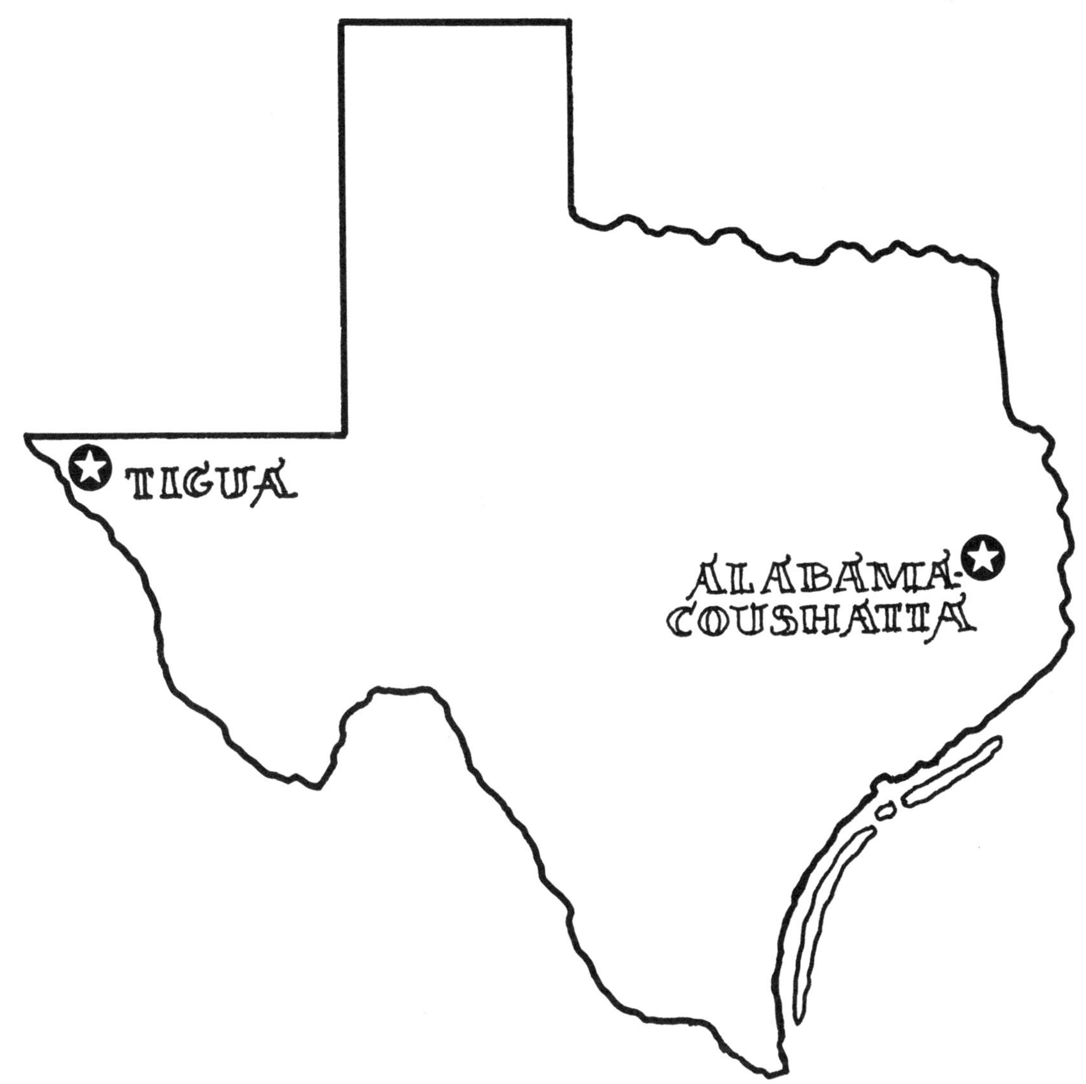

INDIANS TODAY

There are only a few Indians living in Texas today. These tribes came from other states. They live on reservations which are lands set aside for them by the state government. Alabama-Coushatta (ah-lah-bam-ah-coo-SHAH-tuh) Indians live on a reservation near Livingston in East Texas. Another reservation is near El Paso. The Tigua (TEE-wuh) Indians who live there originally came from New Mexico.

REMINDERS of TEXAS INDIANS

In the museums of Texas we can see clothing and belongings of early Indians who lived in Texas. We can still find their arrowheads in the fields and woods. We can still see ancient Indian paintings on cave walls, and we have given Indian names to some of our streets, towns, lakes, and rivers.

But the best reminder we have of the early Indians is the name of our state:

TEXAS is an Indian word which means *FRIENDS*.

CAN YOU REMEMBER?

1. How long ago did the first people come to Texas?
   ____
2. What were they looking for? ____________________
3. Name three crops grown by the Farming Indians.
   ____
4. What is *adobe*? ______________________________
5. Where did the Fishing Indians live? ______________
6. What was the favorite food of the Plant Gatherers?
   ____
7. Name three ways that Hunting Indians used the buffalo. ______________________________________
8. Did all Indians speak the same language? __________
9. What happened to the Indians of Texas? ___________
   ____
10. What does the Indian word "Texas" mean? _________

◆◆◆◆◆◆◆◆◆◆◆◆◆◆◆◆

WHAT CAME FIRST?

Use the numbers 1, 2, 3, 4, 5, to show which event happened first.

____ The first people came into Texas 38,000 years ago.
____ Spaniards brought horses to Texas.
____ Bows and arrows were invented.
____ Indians fought battles with the Europeans who came to Texas
____ Indians went to live on reservations.

◆◆◆◆◆◆◆◆◆◆◆◆◆◆◆◆

IS IT TRUE?

Write a *T* before each sentence which is true.

____ The first Indians came to Texas in a bus.

____ Farming Indians grew corn, pumpkins, and squash.

____ Tepees were made of bricks.

____ Indian children ate chocolate popsicles.

____ Prickly pear cactus was eaten by the Indians.

____ A canoe can be made out of a tree trunk.

____ Early Indians lived in caves.

____ All Indians spoke the same language.

MAKE THEM MATCH

Draw a line from the word to the picture that matches it.

grass hut		drum	
arrow		corn	
tepee		buffalo	
dugout		prickly pear	
bear	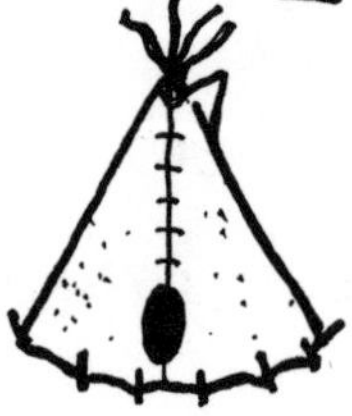	turtle	

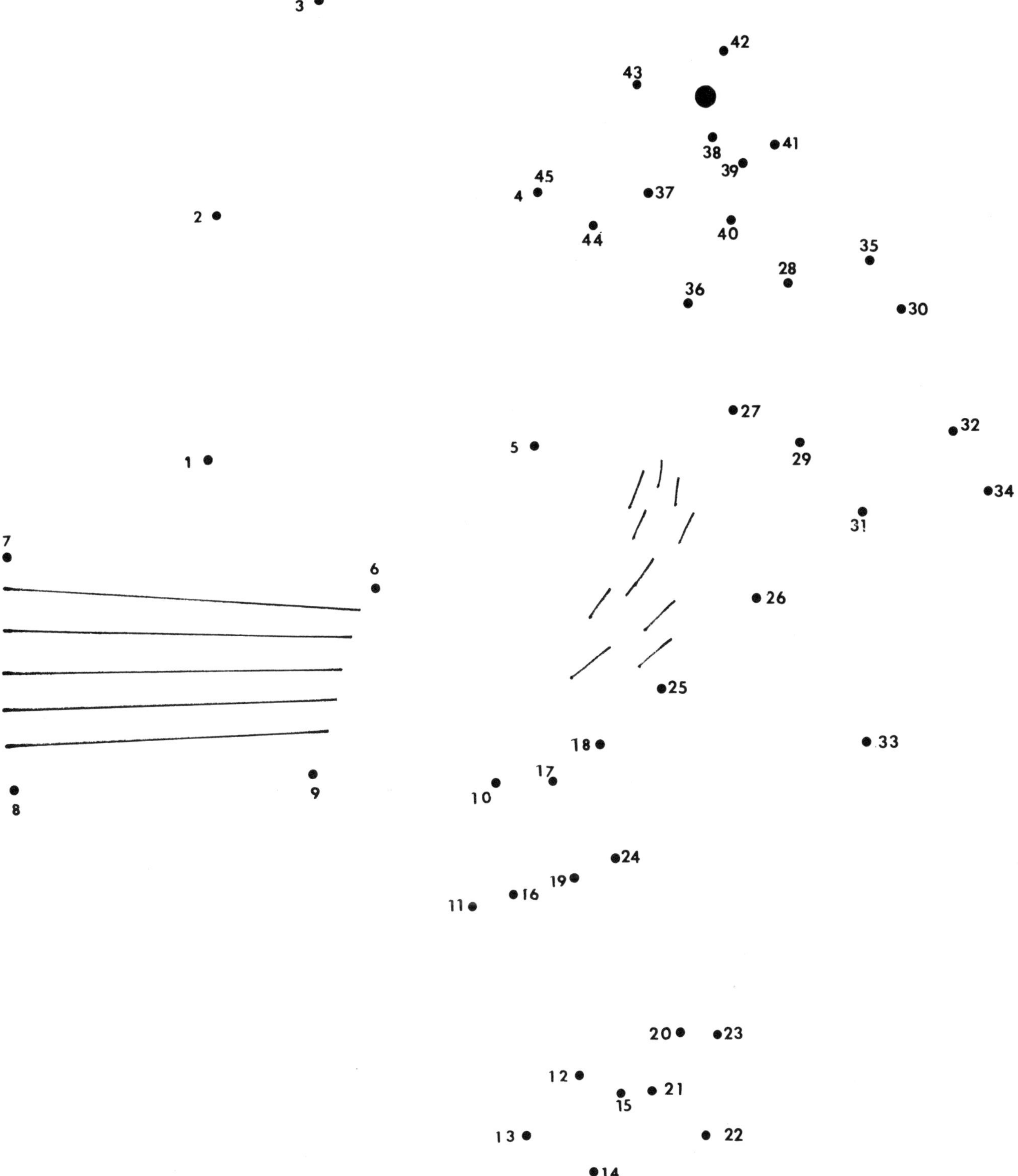

JOIN THE DOTS

. . . and see what an Indian painted on a cliff in Frio Canyon near Leakey, Texas, many hundreds of years ago.

CROSSWORD PUZZLE

ACROSS

1. A prickly plant
2. This makes a dug-out
3. Buffalo hunter
4. Food made from corn

DOWN

1. A slow mover
2. Bow and ______
3. A pointed weapon

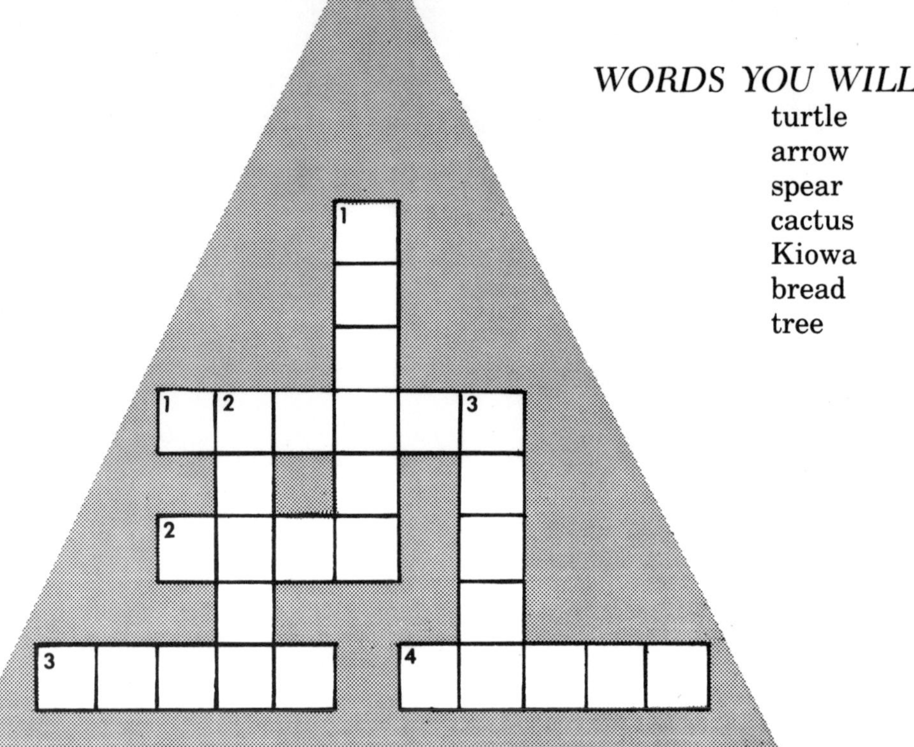

WORDS YOU WILL NEED

turtle
arrow
spear
cactus
Kiowa
bread
tree

ANSWERS

page 29 at top

1—38,000 years; 2—food (animals and plants); 3—corn, beans, squash, pumpkin; 4—a mixture of grass, ashes, dirt, and water; 5—along the Gulf coast; 6—prickly pear cactus; 7—for clothes, food, tepees; 8—no; 9—they died from wars and disease or went to live in Mexico or on reservations; 10—Friends

page 29 at bottom

1, 3, 2, 5, 4

page 30 at top

The *T* goes before 2, 5, 6, 7